MORE SKITS THAT WIN

Also by Ruth Vaughn . . .
Skits That Win

MORE SKITS THAT WIN

BY RUTH VAUGHN

ZONDERVAN
PUBLISHING HOUSE

OF THE ZONDERVAN CORPORATION | GRAND RAPIDS, MICHIGAN 49506

MORE SKITS THAT WIN

© 1977 by The Zondervan Corporation
Grand Rapids, Michigan

Sixth printing 1982

Library of Congress Cataloging in Publication Data

Vaughn, Ruth.
    More skits that win.

    SUMMARY: Eight skits to be performed for and by teenagers for evangelistic
purposes.
        1. Evangelism plays.   [1.   Christian life —
Drama.   2.   Plays]   I.   Title.
BV3795.V38   812'.5'4   77-3461

ISBN 0-310-33671-6

Printed in the United States of America

For
RONNIE
The blue-eyed boy
Whose creativity is my joy
Whose sparkle is my sunshine
Whose walk with Christ is my daily prayer

CONTENTS

INTRODUCTION

Drama has been powerfully used by forces outside the church in their effort to persuade. Surely it is time that we, within the church, utilize this power to present the life-saving, life-transforming good news of the gospel.

This book of skits is written as a tool to help evangelize teenagers for Christ. The effectiveness of these skits in winning people of all ages to Christ has been demonstrated, but their specific focus is upon teens in the crucial decision-making years of their lives.

So use these skits and you will discover that they are interest-catching, mood-setting, and thought-stimulating. Their message will be effective tools in the task of evangelizing youth. This is why they were written.

RUTH VAUGHN

MORE
SKITS
THAT
WIN

THE TEST

Characters

Narrator I: Boy with strong speaking voice
Emily: Beautiful young girl
Esteban: Strong, handsome youth
Narrator II: Girl with expressive speaking voice
Christ Figure
Rich Young Ruler
Soloist

Setting

The stage may be set with potted plants and other greenery to resemble a garden. This setting may be as simple or lavish as desired.

Costuming

Emily should be elegantly dressed; Esteban in plain rough garments. Both are twentieth-century young people. The Rich Young Ruler's clothing should be as elegant as possible, complete with rings and bracelets. The clothing for the Christ Figure should be a simple white flowing robe and sandals. Both, of course, should be dressed in keeping with the biblical period.

Properties

The only properties needed for this skit are optional. If, in the last scene, you choose to spotlight a picture as suggested, you will need the picture, easel, and spot.

Skit

(Narrator enters and stands at extreme stage right.)

Narrator I: Eleanor Mercein Kelly wrote a poignant short story entitled "Basquerie." It tells of a beautiful young woman who has prepared all her life to marry for money. This has been her one goal, her one obsession. During an off-season at an exclusive resort, she finds no eligible wealthy men available. Although she knows it can be only a fleeting relationship, she allows herself to

13

fall in love with a young man who shows no signs of wealth. Ultimately the young man, Esteban Urruty, asks the young woman, Emily Weldon, to go home with him to meet his family. She has some pangs of conscience, knowing she will never marry into his simple life. But doesn't she owe him something for the happiness he has given her in a dull season? Believing she does, she agrees to go with him.

Esteban's family are rural peasant people. They all work in the fields, even the grandmother. Throwing herself into the spirit of the moment, Emily works with them. Emily reads Esteban's pride in her in his eyes. She knows his family has accepted her when the grandmother takes her aside to show her the trousseau of Esteban's mother. She then tells Emily that the trousseau is hers because, like Esteban's mother, Emily is small and uncommon and much-loved.

Emily realizes that her ruse has gone farther than she intended. She cannot possibly marry Esteban although she admits that she loves him. But her goal in life is to marry for wealth. Love has never counted before. It cannot count now. Somehow she has to free herself from this family — somehow she must get away from the beloved but poor Esteban.

But how? How could she publicly announce to the family that she would never think of marrying a lovable peasant? Then she has an idea. The one thing this family will not tolerate is laxity in keeping the marriage laws. She then tells the grandmother she is a divorcée.

In a rage, the grandmother commands her to leave and reprimands Esteban for bringing her home. Emily breaks away from the family and runs from the room. Esteban starts after her. Let us observe the scene.

(Narrator I turns to look at stage. Emily runs onstage, sobbing. Esteban rushes after her and when he reaches her, he grabs her by the shoulder. He whirls Emily around to face him. He is obviously shaken.)

Esteban: This — this is not true? *(He searches Emily's face carefully. Then slowly he speaks, answering himself.)* No — it is not true. It is to my grandmother you have lied. But why? Because you do not wish to marry me?

Emily nods.

Esteban: Did you never wish to marry me?

Emily shakes her head.

Esteban: But why? Why have you done this to me? You love me?

Emily: Oh my dear, can't you see — can't you see how absurd it was to expect a woman like me to live such a life as this — think of me — me, Emily Weldon, living among the cattle, hoeing the fields, handling — handling manure, for all I know! There's enough of it about. *(She laughs hysterically.)* I'm not a woman like your grandmother, Esteban. I'm a lady!

Esteban (searchingly): What is a lady?

Emily: You see? You don't even know the difference. Should I have to cook meals for the farm hands? Why, I've never done a useful thing in my life, and never shall. . . . It's impossible, ridiculous! Girls like me are brought up to be useless. We must marry rich men, my dear — rich, can you understand? As my world counts riches, not as a peasant does, who prides himself on how many cows he keeps, or pigs! Motor cars, country houses, yachts — my own or other people's — those things are necessities to me. . . .

Esteban: More than love?

Emily: I'm not fool enough to expect everything, Esteban. I have to have wealth. I shall have it. At any cost. This patriarchal, pastoral, humble sort of life your family lives — I am not fitted for that sort of thing. It — it is too real for me! I am not able —

Esteban (looking at her sadly, his shoulders sagging with disillusionment): No. I see you are not able. The test was too great.

(Esteban walks heavily offstage left while Emily watches with wistful longing in her eyes, pain in the lines of her body. When he is gone, she, too walks heavily offstage right.)

Narrator I: Emily made her choice. Wealth without love was of more value than love without wealth.

Several weeks later she stood alone on the terrace of her exclusive hotel and watched a beautiful yacht slip away toward open sea. When she asked about it, she was informed that the yacht was the possession of one of the wealthiest men in the world: Esteban Urruty. He had been home for the summer to help his family with

15

the field work as he always did. Newspapers said he had recently married a girl he had known for years. The yacht was taking the rich man and his bride on their honeymoon.

Esteban had said to Emily: "Come unto me." Had she been willing to risk all for love, she would have found fulfillment in life. But when she turned away from his invitation to simple love, she lost everything. The young man had put her to a test too great for her to meet. She was not able.

(Narrator I exits stage right. After a moment, Narrator II enters and stands extreme stage left.)

Narrator II: The physician Luke wrote a poignant short story in twelve verses of Scripture. It is the story of a handsome young man who had prepared all his life to handle wealth. This had been his one goal, his one obsession. But one day he stood in a crowd and listened to special words from a special Man. He intuitively sensed the Truth of the words; he throbbingly felt the power of the Man. He determined to speak to this Christ personally. Let us observe the scene.

(The Christ Figure walks onstage from extreme right. He stands with fingers on a small tree with back to the audience. The Rich Young Ruler enters from stage left and faces the audience.)

Ruler (bows): Good day. I am Jacob of the house of Laban. I was deeply touched by Your words today. Good Master, I very much want to inherit the eternal life of which You speak. But how may I do so?

Christ Figure: You know the commandments. Do not commit adultery. Do not kill. Do not steal. Do not bear false witness. Honor your father and mother.

Ruler: Yes, I know the commandments well. I have kept each of them all of my life.

Christ: You lack only one thing: sell all you have and distribute to the poor. This will assure you treasure in heaven. Then come follow Me.

Ruler: But I can't do that. Don't you see? I am a man born to wealth and power. The lands I own, the slaves I command, the luxury for my family — these things are necessities to me —

Christ: More than love?

Ruler: You do love me. I can read it in Your eyes — feel it in

16

Your smile. I would enjoy walking with You, Good Master. But I'm not fool enough to expect everything from life. I have to have wealth. I suspect that Your command involves not so much the good my wealth would do the poor — but the effect my giving it would have on me.

Christ: He that loseth his life for My sake shall find it.

Ruler: That's a dare, a gamble. My wealth is a sure thing. No, I cannot meet your command. I must live my own way. This pastoral, humble life of service you live — I am not fitted for that sort of thing. It — it is too real for me! I am not able —

Christ: No. I see you are not able. The test was too great.

(Ruler walks slowly, heavily offstage. With shoulders sagging in discouragement, Christ follows.)

Narrator II: The rich young man made his choice. He wanted to direct his own life, live according to self-made rules even at the price of spurning the love of Christ. He refused to believe the paradox Jesus expressed: "He that loseth his life for My sake shall find it."

Christ said to the young man: "Come unto Me." Had he been willing to risk all for love, he would have found fulfillment of life. But when he turned away from the invitation to trusting love, he lost everything. Christ had put him to a test too great for him to meet. He was not able.

(Narrator II steps to center stage.)

Shall we bow our heads?

(Music of "Are Ye Able, Said the Master" begins offstage.)

Jesus Christ is speaking to you tonight. He is saying: "Come unto Me."

Can you feel Him? He is searching you out. Your one goal, your one obsession may have nothing to do with riches. But its meaning is the same to you. Could you dare to risk your dream for Christ's love? Could you dare to believe Christ's words: "He that loseth his life for My sake shall find it?"

In this moment of quietness, you are facing His test. Is it too great for you? Are you able to meet it?

(Narrator may hold prayerful position as soloist sings offstage or Narrator may step offstage as a large picture of Christ is placed center stage on an easel. All houselights are dimmed and the

17

picture is spotlighted as the words of this song are meaningfully and clearly sung.)

"Are ye able," said the Master,
"To be crucified with Me?"
"Yea," the sturdy dreamers answered,
"To the death we follow Thee."

Chorus
"Lord, we are able," Our spirits are Thine,
Remold them, make us, like Thee, divine.
Thy guiding radiance above us shall be,
A beacon to God, to faith and loyalty.

"Are ye able" to relinquish
Purple dreams of power and fame,
To go down into the garden,
Or to die a death of shame?

Chorus

"Are ye able" to remember
When a thief lifts up his eyes,
That his pardoned soul is worthy
Of a place in Paradise?

Chorus

"Are ye able," when the shadows
Close around you with the sod,
To believe that spirit triumphs
To commend your soul to God?

Chorus

"Are ye able?" still the Master
Whispers down eternity,
And heroic spirits answer
Now, as then, in Galilee.

Chorus

Invitation.

The short story "Basquerie" is published in *Stories to Remember* selected by Thomas B. Costain and John Beecroft (Garden City: Doubleday and Company, 1956).

*The song was written by Earl Marlatt, 1926. Music by Harry Mason.

18

I DARE YOU!

Characters

Kay: Teen-age girl
Crowd about the Christ Figure
Bartimaeus: A blind man who begs by the highway
Jabal: Friend of Bartimaeus
Don: Teen-age boy

Setting

The bare stage is all that is necessary. If desired, greenery could be arranged at front and back sides of stage to indicate road edges. Center of stage front and back, however, should remain bare.

Costuming

Kay and Don are dressed as typical older teens of the twentieth century. Other members of the cast should be in biblical garb. The Christ Figure may wear white but He should not be obtrusive enough to stand out in the crowd. Bartimaeus' clothing should be dirty and tattered.

Properties

Bartimaeus should have a cup for his begging. He may also have a staff. Kay should have a Bible.

Skit

(Kay comes on center stage, carrying an open Bible.)

Kay (loudly; facing stage left): Okay, kids, let's take it from the beginning. Remember to speak clearly. When we present this in church on Sunday, I want everyone to be able to hear. Everybody ready?

Voice offstage: Yes, Kay, we're ready.

Another voice offstage: Quit shoving!

Kay: Okay, kids. Here goes.

(She moves to extreme stage left and begins to read.)

Kay: "And they came to Jericho. . . ."

(A crowd of people come onstage with the tall Christ Figure

in the center. The Christ Figure should never be seen clearly by the audience, but they should know specifically who he is and where.)

Kay: "And as he went out of Jericho with his disciples and a great number of people . . ."

(Bartimaeus comes onstage, faltering, groping with his hands or cane. He finds the back of center stage and sits cross-legged and arranges his cup.)

Kay: "Blind Bartimaeus, the son of Timaeus, sat by the highway side begging."

(Group moves a bit closer to Bartimaeus. There should be murmuring and typical movement in the crowd.)

Bartimaeus: Who is coming? Who is coming?

Jabal (breaking away from the crowd and going to Bartimaeus): Jesus of Nazareth is coming, Bartimaeus. Think of it! He is walking through Jericho!

Kay: "And when he heard that it was Jesus of Nazareth, he began to cry out, and say. . ."

Bartimaeus: "Jesus, thou son of David, have mercy on me."

(Two others break from crowd. They and Jabal try to shush Bartimaeus.)

Kay: "And many charged him that he should hold his peace: but he cried the more a great deal."

Bartimaeus: Thou son of David, have mercy on me!

(Crowd, which has been moving slowly, stops.)

Kay: "And Jesus stood still, and commanded . . ."

Christ: "Bring the man to me."

Kay: "And they called the blind man, saying unto him . . ."

Jabal (touching Bartimaeus' shoulder): Be of good comfort, rise; he calleth thee.

Kay: "And he, casting away his garment, rose, and came to Jesus."

(Bartimaeus throws aside a top shawl and stands. Jabal helps him to Jesus.)

Kay: "And Jesus answered and said unto him. . . ."

Christ: What wilt thou that I should do unto thee?

Kay: "The blind man said unto him . . ."

Bartimaeus: Lord, that I might receive my sight.

Kay: "And Jesus said unto him . . ."

Christ: Go thy way; thy faith hath made thee whole.

Kay: "And immediately he received his sight, and followed Jesus in the way."

(Bartimaeus is taken into the crowd so he is no longer visible to the audience and the entire crowd moves offstage.)

(Don comes onstage right. Kay meets him center stage.)

Kay: Well — it still needs a lot more work, but I think they're beginning to portray the story effectively, don't you?

Don: I suppose. If that's the kind of thing you want to do.

Kay: Well, what on earth do you mean by that?

Don: No offense. It's just that — well, church groups have been acting out Bible stories since the beginning of time!

Kay: And that's bad?

Don: Well, it surely could be better.

Kay: You mean the story?

Don: Well, yes, if you're going to push me. I mean — look — is it really credible that *anyone* in his right mind would ask a blind man what he wanted most in all the world? I mean — now really — isn't that perfectly obvious?

Kay: Yes, it is perfectly obvious that the man is blind. But wait a minute! You're missing the whole point. Bartimaeus was a *man;* not a robot. He had a disability, but he was still a human being. He had to recognize his condition before Jesus could do anything for him.

Don (frowns): Now hold on!

Kay: It's true, Don. Facts can only answer the questions we pose and if we do not ask the right questions we cannot get the right answers.

Don: You mean if he had refused to ask —

Kay: He would not have received. Which is the precise reason that you do not receive.

Don: Do not receive what?

Kay: Answers to your search for Truth. Light for your blindness.

(Don looks disgusted and walks away from her. Kay follows.)

Kay: Oh, Don, don't you see? You are blind, too — not physically, but spiritually. You seek Truth, but you cannot find.

Don: And if I would ask, Christ could heal my blindness as surely as He did Bartimaeus' in the first century A.D.? If I would ask Him, He would fulfill my search for Truth?

Kay: He would.

(Don turns to her.)

Don: Kay, are you really as naïve as you sound? Do you believe everything you hear — everything you read?

Kay: No.

Don (searches her face carefully): Well, then, why do you stand there so self-assured and make such preposterous promises?

Kay: Because He did those miracles for me.

(She sings)

> Christ's love is like warm golden sunshine
> Which touches all parts of me;
> The glow never leaves; it drives out the cold.
> He cares for the blind and the searching.

> Christ's voice is like a whisper from heaven
> It's always definite and clear,
> And when His Voice comes, we know it is Truth.
> He cares for the blind and the searching.

> So there is no more fear of losing myself
> In the midst of a mob of humanity;
> For I've found myself in Someone bigger than I
> Who's restored all my reason and sanity.

> Christ walks with me when it is storming;
> He stands with me when stars shine bright.
> In a world of confusion and fear and doubt,
> He's there with the blind and the searching.

Don (musingly): Ask and it shall be given . . . *(he whirls suddenly)* . . . But I have asked!

Kay: For what?

Don: For *what?* For Light. For Truth.

Kay: On whose terms?

Don: I don't know what you mean.

(He turns away from her.)

22

Kay: I think you do. You want Light in specific areas of your choice. You want Truth in your own way, structured to fit your mold. You *really* asked for self. And you received.

Don (whirling back to her; speaking with intensity): I asked for Truth.

Kay: On His terms?

Don: What are His terms?

Kay: Total commitment of your own free will — *of* your own free will.

Don: What do you mean by the repetition?

Kay: No repetition. Christ's demands are that you stand *unchained,* with perfect liberty to do your *own* will, but you deliberately *choose* to submit your will to His.

(Don walks away thoughtfully.)

Kay: Don, you do not commit your own free will by divine coercion. You commit it *of* your own free will. Because you love — because you want to serve.

Don (turns): That's pretty stiff!

Kay: Those are His terms. Don, you can find light; you can find Truth whenever you ask for it — on His terms.

Don: I don't know if I can do that. I don't know if I'm strong enough.

Kay: Don, *try!*

Don: Am I, of my own free will, able to crucify myself, surrender my own desires and goals, abandon *my* plan for *His?*

Kay: The plan Christ has for your life is a beautiful one, Don. With your youth, your intelligence, your ability, you could make an important contribution to the world in which we live.

(Don studies Kay a moment, then takes a deep shuddering breath and turns to pace the stage.)

Don: I can't, Kay. I can't.

(Kay rushes to him.)

Kay: Don, if you will dare to lose yourself — you will find a much better self in Christ.

Don: If I dare! If I dare!

(He walks to center stage and expressively sings.)

Don: If I dare to do His will
  In the conflict of this hour . . .

If I dare to do His will
I'd come to know His saving power.

If I dare to give my love
He would make my life worthwhile;
I could know peace from above
And the wonder of His smile.

So much courage it would take;
Not a weakling could I be!
So much difference it would make
If I *dared* to offer *me!*

If I dare to do His will
In the conflict of this hour . . .
If I dare to do His will
I'd come to know His saving power . . .
If I dare . . .
                 If I dare . . .
                      If I dare!*

(Instrumental music continues)

Kay: You're right, Don. If you dare to choose to live for the hard right over the easy wrong. It takes courage and strength of character to be a Christian. You — and all youth alive today — who have felt the call of Christ understand that Christ will bring to you the answer for your search for Truth. . . . He will give you light to replace the blindness if you ask. You know that . . . so that is not the issue. The issue is: Do you have the courage to *dare* to lose yourself to find it again in Someone bigger than yourself?

Don: Truth on His terms?

Kay: Truth on *your* terms will take your purity, your ability, your dreams and destroy them. Truth on your terms will leave you always with a broken heart and self-contempt. Truth on *His* terms is the only way.

(She sings pleadingly.)

Kay: "Will you dare?" asks the Master
          "To be crucified with Me?

*These words may be sung to the music of "Hallelujah! What a Saviour!" written by Philipp Bliss in 1902.

24

Won't you come in surrender
Saying: 'Yes, I will follow Thee'?''
Don (sings): So much courage it does take;
Not a weakling can I be!
So much difference it will make
I will *dare* to offer *me!*
(He takes a step and lifts his face to sing his earnest commitment.)
I will dare to do Your will
Not a coward will I be.
I will dare to do Your will;
Take me, Master. Take all of me.
I will dare . . .
I will dare . . .
I will dare!

Invitation

THE PERIL OF RELUCTANCE

Characters

Dana: Teen-age girl
Judy: Teen-age girl
Dinah: Maid in Dana's home
Adam: Butler in Dana's home

Setting

Both scenes are in front of Dana's home. There should be a door in center of stage. On each side of the door should be a planter with greenery, flowers, etc. Artificial grass with a path leading up to the door would lend atmosphere, if desired. There could also be windows. There should be a bench sitting about midway on stage right.

Costuming

Dana and Judy are dressed in typical teen-age attire. Dinah and Adam should be dressed in uniforms depicting their stations in the household.

Properties

Dana and Judy should have printed programs in first scene. Judy will need schoolbooks to carry in second scene.

Skit

SCENE I

(Dana and Judy come onstage. They carry printed programs.)

Dana: Wow! What a terrific program, Judy!

Judy: I know — and oh, man! that third soloist sounded like Gabriel!

Dana (grinning slyly): Um hmm!

Judy (still ecstatic and not noticing Dana): And he looked like an angel, too!

Dana (laughs): I was wondering when you'd get around to your *real* sentiments!

Judy: What — I mean — why — I only mean I thought he was a *very* good soloist.

27

Dana: Good — and oh! so handsome!

Judy: All right. Tease me. But first — tell me who he is!

Dana: Didn't you know? He is the oldest son of our minister.

Judy: Really? I thought Mark was an only child.

Dana: Nope. He has a brother. He's been away in college. That's why you haven't seen him before. His name is Geron.

Judy: Reeeeallly?

Dana: Um hmm. He plans to be a minister.

Judy: Oh! *(The girls go to the bench and sit.)* Does Mark plan to be a minister, Dana?

Dana: I don't think so. He hopes to be a doctor — a missionary doctor, I believe. Mark is a terrific Christian.

Judy: He is very nice.

Dana: Geron is too — and oh! so handsome!

Judy: Dana, cut it out. I especially enjoyed his solo in the cantata tonight. That's all. If I didn't go to church for any other reason, I would go to hear the choir sing.

(Dana looks at Judy, frowning.)

Judy: Oh — oh well, I go to church for other reasons, of course — and I'm quite faithful too — but if there were no other reasons, I'd go just to hear the choir. Is that so bad?

Dana: No. But I have been wondering, Judy. What *are* the reasons you go to church?

Judy: Oh — I — *(she laughs nervously)* — I don't know really. I've never thought about it. *(She thinks a moment.)* Oh — I go — well, I go because my parents go and because they want me with them. And I go because — you go — and all of the other kids who are my friends. Why do you ask? Aren't those the reasons you go to church?

Dana: Well — those *are* reasons, of course. But the *real* reason I go to church is something much deeper than those things.

Judy: The fact that you're a Christian?

Dana: Uh huh. The fact that — that I love Jesus Christ more than anything or anyone else in the world. And when I go to church, I can worship Him, I can pray to Him, I can receive His guidance from God's Word and the pastor's message. I feel a compelling desire to go to church — for intensely personal reasons. Can you understand that, Judy?

28

Judy: I guess so.

Dana: Judy — when are you going to become a Christian? When are you going to allow Christ to enter your heart and fill your life with His love and guidance?

Judy (rising nervously and walking about): Oh — I don't know. Sometime I will.

Dana (rising and going to her): But Judy — why do you keep putting it off? The Bible says: Now is the day of salvation; now is the accepted time. Why not make a decision for Christ *now?*

Judy: Oh — I don't know really — I just don't want to do anything that drastic yet.

Dana: But why?

Judy: Well — it's such an important decision. It changes one's life so very much and — I — well — I am just in no hurry to make it. I know I will have to sometime, Dana. I promise I will. But — not yet, Dana. Not now.

Dana: But Judy, it's dangerous to put off this decision. You said yourself it was important . . . that it is life-changing. So the sooner it is made — the better off you are.

Judy: Well — maybe so. I will think about it. Honest I will.

Dana: But why not now? We can kneel right here. Together. You can accept Jesus as your Savior tonight.

Judy: No — not now, Dana. I — I'm not ready now. Please don't press me.

(Dana lowers her head. Curtain. If no curtain available, Dana gives Judy a quick hug and they exit stage right, stage left.)

SCENE II

(Judy comes on stage humming and carrying some schoolbooks.)

Judy (taking a deep breath): Oh — it's a beautiful morning! Entirely too nice to go to school and study books!

(Judy goes to door and knocks.)

Judy (calling): Dana, my friend, you had best be up and ready! We're going to have to make tracks this lovely day to beat the tardy bell.

(The door is opened. Dinah comes on stage.)

Judy: Oh good morning, Dinah. Have you taken Adam's place at the door after all these years? Where is Dana?

Dinah (very agitated and upset): Oh, Miss Judy — that's just the problem! Miss Dana — Miss Dana — she's gone! She's gone and we can't find any trace of her anywhere!

Judy (frowning): Gone? Dana? Where?

Dinah: Miss Judy, I'm tryin' to tell you. We don't know where. She is just gone! I went into her room this morning and she was sleeping so peacefully. The way she does with her arms flung out like wings of an angel on the bed. I awoke her and she sat up, rubbed her eyes, and told me that she wanted pancakes and blueberry syrup for breakfast. And so I left and went to make the pancakes. And while I was making the pancakes, Dana's mother and father came into the room and ordered their breakfast. Then they went out into the sitting room to read the morning papers like they allus do. When the pancakes wuz ready, I went to call Miss Dana. And — she was gone! She was gone! Her dress was laid out on the bed — but she — Miss Dana was gone!

(She puts her hands over her face and walks distractedly about stage. Judy watches her in complete bewilderment.)

When I realized she wasn't in the shower or anywhere, I ran down to the sitting room to tell her parents — and Miss Judy! — they wuz gone, too!

Judy: Her parents were gone?

Dinah: Yes'm. Just like that! It hadn't been five minutes since I had heard them talkin' over the mornin' paper. And just that quick! *(she clicks her fingers)* — they wuz gone!

Judy: Oh now, Dinah, there has to be some explanation. Maybe — maybe they — well, went somewhere suddenly.

Dinah: Their car is here and none of them wuz dressed yet. Where would they go in their robes and house slippers? And why wouldn't they tell me?

Judy: I — well — I don't know.

(There is the sound of running feet offstage.)

Adam (offstage): Dinah! Dinah! Where are you? Dinah! Dinah! Where are you?

Dinah: Out here, Adam.

(Adam enters, breathlessly.)

Adam: Dinah — they're all gone! Every one of them is gone!

Judy: Who is gone, Adam?

Adam: Our minister, Miss Judy — and every member of his family! I went into the house and there was food on the table and food on the plates. It was still warm — but they were gone! The Rev. and Mrs., Mark, and Geron — they were all gone! I walked out of the house and met a policeman. He was standing on the corner — kinda in a daze. I went up to him and asked if he had seen the Reverend. He said: "I haven't seen anyone I was supposed to!" I asked what he meant and he said they had had forty car wrecks reported in the last twenty minutes — and half of the cars didn't have drivers!

Judy: Didn't have drivers! *(rolls her eyes and turns away in disgust)* Why that's insane!

Adam: That's what the policeman said, Miss Judy. But he said it was true anyhow! He said when there was a collision and the police went to investigate, there would be no driver in at least one of the cars.

Judy: Maybe they left the scene of the accident. That happens.

Adam: Forty times in twenty minutes in one small town? And many of the people involved in the accidents didn't see drivers in the other cars at the time of impact — none of them saw the other drivers walk away!

Judy: Well, there has to be some explanation. There just has to be.

Adam: Yes, ma'am. There has to be.

(He sighs heavily and goes over to sit on the bench. He puts his head in his hands.)

Dinah: Dana and her parents, the Reverend and his family, the drivers of all those cars — it surely do sound like the Second Coming of the Lord!

Judy (startled): Dinah! Don't be funny now!

Dinah: I wasn't being funny, Miss Judy. What else could explain this?

Judy: Well, I don't know right now — but I certainly know it isn't anything as ridiculous as that! All those bumper stickers on cars warning that they will be driverless at the Second Coming — they are just for fun! Why — that's impossible! Anyway — it couldn't be true because — because we're here.

Adam (heavily): I know.

Judy: Oh, now, Adam! Don't be like that. You know it isn't true! Why — it's so sudden — without warning or anything — *(her voice trails off)*

Adam: The Bible says in Mark 13:32,33: "But of that day and that hour knoweth no man, no, not the angels which are in heaven, neither the Son, but the Father. Take ye heed, watch and pray: for ye know not when the time is."

Judy (taken aback): Yes, of course, it does say that — but it can't mean now — I mean — we're here! Isn't that proof enough? Why — I go to church every Sunday — every Sunday I go to church! *(turns desperately to Dinah)* And you go to church too, Dinah, and you pay your tithe. I know you do. *(turns to Adam)* And Adam — why you can quote more Scripture and give chapter and verse than anyone I know! Why — we would have been taken! Of course we would have. Don't you see? Of course we would have!

Adam (sadly): Going to church on Sunday, paying your tithe — and even quoting Scripture isn't enough, Miss Judy. There has to be a personal contract between you and the Lord Jesus. Nobody else can do it for you — and no matter how good you are — or how much you go to church — and do all of those other things — if your heart isn't right with the Lord — then you can't be eligible for His coming!

Judy: Why — but — that means — that I'm lost! That means that Jesus — has — come — and taken His children with Him — and I am left behind!

(She walks toward center stage. The full import of the moment is dawning upon her and she is horrified.)

Judy (looking desperately at Dinah): It can't be! *(Dinah lowers her head sadly. Judy believes. The importance of her acting here is of utmost importance.)* But it is! I had an opportunity just last night to accept Jesus as my personal Savior. I refused. But — I didn't *mean* to be lost! I told Dana that I was going to be a Christian. I even promised. But I just wasn't quite ready then —

(Judy looks at Dinah and Adam. Dinah stands dejectedly with head bowed. Adam sits on bench, head in hands. Judy looks at them, her eyes still pleading for assurance that it is not true. Then she raises her eyes toward the heavens.)

Judy: I intended to become a Christian. You know I did. I even promised I would. *(She lowers her eyes as she realizes the futility of the prayer.)* But intentions are not enough! And now it's too late! Eternally too late.

(Curtain. If no curtain, Judy slowly and dejectedly walks back to sit with Adam. All three characters hold pose as leader gives the invitation.)

I WANT TO LIVE!

Characters

Male soloist
Hidden male voice
Cheryl: teen-age girl

Setting

Stage is bare except for a large picture of the "Christ on the Cross" painted by Peter Paul Rubens. This may be acquired at your local library or borrowed from a local bookstore. The picture should be placed on an easel draped with red or black velvet for greater effectiveness.

Costuming

Cheryl should be smartly dressed in the latest fashion.

Skit

Music begins softly: "I Gave My Life for Thee" (Frances R. Havergal) as lights are slowly dimmed to a moment of total darkness. Spotlight comes up slowly, focusing full on picture. After a few moments, Cheryl walks onstage and stands at side looking at the picture. Male soloist sings offstage.)

> *Soloist:* I gave My life for thee,
> My precious blood I shed,
> That thou might'st ransomed be
> And quickened from the dead;
> I gave, I gave My life for thee.
> What hast thou given for Me?
> I gave, I gave My life for thee.
> What hast thou given for Me?
>
> My Father's house of light,
> My glory-circled throne
> I left, for earthly night,
> For wanderings sad and lone;
> I left, I left it all for thee.
> Hast thou left aught for Me?
> I left, I left it all for thee,
> Hast thou left aught for Me?

I suffered much for thee,
　　More than thy tongue can tell,
Of bitterest agony,
　　To rescue thee from hell;
I've borne, I've borne it all for thee.
　　What hast thou borne for Me?
I've borne, I've borne it all for thee.
　　What hast thou borne for Me?

And I have brought to thee,
　　Down from My home above,
Salvation full and free,
　　My pardon and My love;
I bring, I bring rich gifts to thee.
　　What hast thou brought to Me?
I bring, I bring rich gifts to thee.
　　What hast thou brought to Me?

(Instrumental music continues. Cheryl moves a step closer to the picture. She is studying it intently.)

Voice: I have chosen you, and ordained you that ye should go and bring forth fruit.

Cheryl (startled): What?

Voice: I have chosen you, and ordained you that ye should go and bring forth fruit.

Cheryl: Lord? (*Looks around her. Shakes herself as if to wake from a dream. Then — in an effort to explain to anyone looking on*) I — I am just looking at the picture. It is a masterpiece of art. I — I am not personally involved.

Voice: I gave *my* life for you. *I* was personally involved.

Cheryl (obviously shaken; steps closer to the picture): Lord?

Voice: I have chosen you.

Cheryl (accepting the Voice as the Lord): Well — yes — but you see —

Voice: You have not chosen Me.

Cheryl: We-ll — I'm all *for* You, Lord. You're just not *in* me yet.

Voice: I have chosen you.

Cheryl: It's not — that — I'm not willing — really — it's just that — I'm too small! You see — were I to choose You to dwell *in* me — there would be no room for — *me* — at all!

Voice: That's the whole idea.

36

Cheryl (takes a deep breath): Yes, I know. That's the whole idea. For You to dwell *in* me, I'd have to crucify my own selfish nature — and I'm not ready to do that yet. *(Her words are faltering; she is seeking to choose carefully.)* It's not that I don't care about You. It's just that — well — there are many things that *I* want to do — that *I* want to experience — that *I* want to participate in — and I know I could not were I to — choose — to ask You to dwell *in* me.

(Cheryl turns and walks to edge of stage right. That she is suffering should be evident in her acting. Her head is bowed in meditation. Then she wheels and walks back toward the picture.)

Cheryl: I want You to understand. At my age — I want to *live!* To the fullest. Someday I will choose You. But not just now. I — I want to *live!*

Voice: I did not live. I *died*.

(Cheryl lowers her head into her hands. She turns from the picture.)

Voice: But in My death was life — life for Me — life for you — life for all mankind. I found My life by losing it. And you, Cheryl — if you would be crucified afresh with Me, you would find *life* in the cup of death, and drinking it, you would win *life* forevermore!

Cheryl (turning back toward picture): How can I be sure?

Voice: Because *I am the Truth*.

Cheryl: But even without *me,* I'm awfully small. Could I ever be large enough for *You?*

Voice: No. But I can reach out to other lives through you — in the overflow.

Cheryl: And they, too, could win *life* forevermore?

Voice: I have chosen you, and ordained you that you should go and bring forth fruit.

Cheryl (kneeling, sings):

> Into my heart, into my heart
> Come into my heart, Lord Jesus;
> Come in today, come in to stay,
> Come into my heart, Lord Jesus.

>   (Harry D. Clarke)

(Cheryl holds pose; instrumental music continues.)
Invitation.

IS THAT ALL THERE IS?

Characters

Donna: A sophisticated professional singer

Setting

The living room of Donna's apartment. The stage may be impressionistically set with only a few pieces of furniture or it may be realistically set with backdrops of wallpaper, curtains, full furnishings.

Costuming

Donna's attire is optional; whatever is chosen should be sophisticated and typical of a professional singer. A housecoat would be appropriate. She wears earrings.

Properties

Record player on which she will pretend to play the background music to her singing. She will need a Bible in which is a slip of paper. A telephone is necessary.

Skit

(Scene opens with phone ringing. Donna enters briskly and picks up the receiver. She removes an earring, puts the receiver to her ear.)

Donna: Hello. . . . yes, I am up! Not because I want to be — but because I am a hard worker! *(She laughs and "listens" a moment.)* Yes, I have the number down all right. *("Listens")* Yes, I'm sure. I know Jerry is ill, but he made a record of it before he went home. I've been practicing with the record. Aren't you impressed? *("Listens" and laughs heartily)* Well, you ought to be impressed! If you're not now, you will be when you hear me sing it. *("Listens")* I do a great job. I ought to — the words of that song express exactly the way I feel — if ever I do a great job on a song — it ought to be that one. *(Her manner changes from laughter to sadness. She "listens" a moment more.)* Yeah — okay. Good-by.

(Donna hangs up the receiver and stands there for a moment with her hands on the phone.)

Donna: If ever I do a great job on a song —

(She sighs and walks slowly over to the phonograph and puts on a record. Music begins offstage. She walks back to center stage and begins to sing with expression.)

Donna: (Sings) "Is That All There Is?"

(After Donna sings, instrumental music continues softly. Donna walks over and flings herself on the couch. After a moment, she sits up and reaches for the Bible lying on the table almost covered with magazines.)

Donna: Mother's Bible. I am a sentimental jerk to keep that on my table. *(She smiles as she opens the Book.)* Still she loved it. Oddly enough, it gave meaning to her life. I tried it. I really did for awhile. But after mother died, it just didn't work for me. *(She flips casually through the pages.)* And so far as I know — it doesn't work for anyone else. I've traveled all over — and watched the man with his bed of coals — the man with spikes to walk on — the woman burning her jade sticks — the woman curtsying to the Virgin. I watched them all — and when they turned away from all of that, their eyes were still lonely — their smiles were still thin. They didn't find more. *(She sighs heavily.)* Neither did I.

(Donna turns more pages — and then finds the slip of paper folded. Curiously, she opens it.)

Donna: It's mother's handwriting. How odd! I never saw this before. I wonder what it is. *(She looks at it carefully, then begins to read slowly, wonderingly.)*

"I've always had a feeling — ever since I was a little girl — that there must be more to life than I found." *(Donna frowns and scrutinizes the paper carefully. Then with puzzlement, she speaks)* Mother? Mother felt there was more to life? How strange! She always seemed so assured, so contented!

(Donna pauses and meditates for a moment. Then she returns to the letter.) "I had almost given up when one day I found the answer to life. It was very simple really — but I had never known it before. When I found it, my whole life changed."

(Donna grimaces at the letter and impatiently addresses it.) Well — don't talk about it — tell what it is.

(She returns to the letter.) "I discovered that Christianity was not a philosophy, not a dogma, not a creed. I discovered that Christianity was a Personality — a vibrant, beautiful, *living* Personality: Jesus Christ.

"When I met Him, He did not make an impression on me. He made a life-change. And I knew, in every fiber of my being, that there truly was *more* to life. And I had found it. In Him.

"He gave me a new life, a new self, a new consciousness of moral reality, a new exuberance, a new — ever-ringing — song! He gave me *more* to life than I had ever dreamed could be.

"I am forgiven and saved by an act which saves the world — and gives me moral power to confront the world — and to surmount it — and to live, not somehow, but *triumphantly*. Jesus Christ did all this for me. But not for me only. But for *whosoever will.*"

(Slowly Donna lets the slip of paper fall into her lap. She repeats the words almost as if in a trance.)

Donna: But not for me only. But for *whosoever will*. I learned that in Sunday school when I was a kid. "For God so loved the world that he gave his only begotten son that *whosoever* believeth in him shall not perish but have everlasting life."

(Donna places the Bible on the table and rises to pace about the stage.)

Donna: "I discovered that Christianity was not a philosophy," *(she reads from the paper)* "not a dogma, not a creed. Christianity is a Personality — a vibrant, beautiful, *living* Personality: Jesus Christ." Funny, I went to church all my life as a kid — and I never knew that before either. Somehow in all the stately creeds, in all the homiletic skill, Jesus Christ got lost for me.

(She walks back to the table and picks up the Bible. She opens it and reads.)

Donna: "I am come a light into the world, that whosoever believeth on me should not abide in darkness." *(turns the page)* "I am the door: by me if any man enter in, he shall be saved and shall go in and out, and find pasture." "I am the good shepherd: the good shepherd giveth his life for the sheep." "My sheep hear my voice, and I know them, and they follow me: and I give unto them eternal life." *(she turns page)* "Jesus saith unto her, Said I not

41

unto thee, that, if thou wouldest believe, thou shouldest see the glory of God?'' *(She paces for a moment thoughtfully.)* The glory of God. That would surely make life complete. No wonder there has been an emptiness — if I were created to live with a Personality who would show me the glory of God!

(She sings.) IS THAT ALL THERE IS? *(She shakes her head and smiles as she answers.)* No, that's not all there is. There is the Personality, Jesus Christ. And I am ready to meet Him.

(Donna lays the Bible down and kneels. The music softly modulates from the pensive refrain of the first song into the music of Nevin's "My Rosary." Prayerfully, expressively, Donna sings these words to the music.)

Donna: Just as I am, Thine own to be,
Friend of the young, who lovest me,
To consecrate myself to Thee,
    O Jesus Christ, I come.
    O Jesus Christ, I come.

In the glad morning of my day
My life to give, my vows to pay,
With no reserve and no delay,
    With all my heart I come.
    With all my heart I come.

I would live ever in the light,
I would work ever for the right,
I would serve Thee with all my might,
    Therefore, to Thee I come.
    Therefore, to Thee I come.

Just as I am, young, strong, and free,
To be the best that I can be
For truth and righteousness and Thee,
Lord of my life, I come. Amen

(Marianne Farningham, 1887)

(Donna holds pose; instrumental music continues.)

Invitation.

"Is That All There Is?" may be purchased in sheet music form from your local music store or may be ordered from West Coast Publications, Inc., 4321 West Jefferson Boulevard, Los Angeles, California 90016. It may also be purchased as a recording by Peggy Lee on Capitol Records.

THERE'S MYSELF TO THINK ABOUT!

Characters

Gary: Teen-age boy
Ronnie: Teen-age boy
Manoah: Samson's father
Zepha: Samson's mother
Samson: Strongest man
Antonio Stradivarius: violin maker

Setting

The stage should represent a garden. This may be as impressionistically or realistically developed as desired. There should be a couple of benches and a table.

Costuming

Gary and Ronnie wear typical twentieth century dress. Manoah, Zepha, Samson wear biblical dress. Antonio Stradivarius wears typical eighteenth century dress.

Properties

Tall stools will be necessary for Gary and Ronnie. A mixing bowl will be needed for Zepha, and a violin and bow for Stradivarius.

Skit

(Ronnie enters, carrying his stool. He places it outside the curtain at extreme stage right. Ronnie sits.)

Ronnie: Riots in Algiers
Conservation in Maine
The Wall in Germany . . .

Rock Operas
Fallout
The man in space
Ban the Bomb
Freedom Riders . . .

This is my world.

Nuclear blast
Radiation
Cancer
Death
Genes

This is my world.

"Ask not what your country can do for you," said JFK.
"Ask what you can do for your country."

But really — there's nothing I can do — and anyway —
There's myself to think about!

Men hating each other
Men selling their houses because a man of another color
bought the house next door
Men blasting public buildings . . .

Men fighting
Across fences
In homes
In the street
In Viet Nam . . .

This is my world.

John F. Kennedy
Robert F. Kennedy
Martin Luther King
die
Israelis at the Olympics
die
the man in a saloon-fight
dies . . .

This is my world.

"For this is the message that ye heard from the beginning,"
said John the Beloved Apostle,
"that we should love one another."

But really — How can I love others? — and anyway —
There's myself to think about!

(Gary enters, carrying his stool. He speaks as he sits.)

Gary: I've been listening to your soliloquy. You sound a lot like Samson.

Ronnie: Like who?

Gary: Don't you ever read the Bible? Don't you know who was the strongest man that ever lived?

Ronnie: Sure. Samson.

Gary: You sound like him.

Ronnie: Would you be so kind as to tell me *what* you are talking about?

Gary: I've got a better idea! Just shut up and listen.

(Curtains open. If no curtains available, characters walk on and off stage at appropriate times.)

(Zepha comes onstage with a bowl in her hands. Manoah follows her and sits on bench. Zepha puts bowl on table and begins to knead dough with her hands.)

Manoah: Where is Samson?

Zepha: He hasn't come home yet.

Manoah: Do you know where he went?

Zepha (sighs): No. He didn't say.

Manoah: But you *know?*

Zepha (nods): Yes. I know.

Manoah (sighs heavily): I don't know what to do with him. I don't know.

(Footsteps and whistling are heard offstage. Zepha looks up eagerly.)

Zepha: Maybe he's here! *(calls)* Samson, is that you?

(Samson enters.)

Samson: It surely is! Your handsome son, Samson, has returned to the home of his birth. *(He gives his mother a bear hug.)* Man! Am I glad to see you! I'm starved. *(He grins at her, teasing, and pokes his finger in the bowl.)* What are you making for your famous son? *(He turns to Manoah.)* Hi, dad! The story of my catching the foxes, setting fire to their tails, and turning them loose in the cornfields of our enemies has made me quite a hero. I told the reporters that you taught me how to tie foxes' tails together! They are most impressed!

45

Zepha: Samson, where have you been?

Samson (walks over to the other bench and sits): Does it matter? I've been having fun.

Manoah (rises): Yes, it matters. You know it matters. We've tried to explain this to you before, Samson. What you do — what you become is very important — not only to us — but to our country — to God!

Samson: Oh, come on, dad! Don't go into it again. I'm sick of it.

Manoah: Well, don't be sick of it! It's a truth you have to face one day!

Samson: I'm trying to deliver Israel. With foxes wagging tails of fire! *(He laughs uproariously.)*

Manoah: This was a good feat in its place. But Samson, you can't keep playing games! You have to face the responsibility that you were born with.

Samson: Well, I didn't ask to be born with it. I don't want the responsibility!

Zepha: But Samson, you're special.

Samson (sarcastically): Tell me about it.

Manoah: You've heard it since your birth. But I think you should hear it again.

Samson: Oh, boy!

Manoah: Zepha, tell him.

Zepha (going to Samson, speaking with love, tenderness, pleading): Samson, you are special. Don't you understand? Before I even knew of your conception, an angel of God appeared to me and told me that you were to grow up to be the man to deliver Israel out of the hand of the Philistines. You, my child, were to be used of God for the good of all mankind. I was so frightened at the thought — and so proud!

Manoah: When your mother told me of the words of the angel, I was as frightened as she. I prayed that God would send him back so he could tell us how to raise you. And God did.

Zepha: He came to me one day in the field and I ran for Manoah.

Manoah: And I asked him face to face: How shall we name the child and how shall we do unto him?

46

Zepha: And the angel told us, Samson. And we followed His every command. Samson, we have done everything we know to make you realize how special you are . . . how much responsibility is yours. . . . O Samson! have we failed?

Samson (rising and walking about impatiently): No, mother, I assure you that you and father have not failed. You have made me intensely aware of my "specialness". . . of my responsibility to my fellow-man and to God — there's only one thing you forget.

Zepha: What is that, Samson?

Samson: I've got myself to think about!

(Curtain. If no curtain available, Samson strides off in anger. Manoah and Zepha look at each other in despair, then heavily follow Samson.)

Gary: You know the rest of the story. He failed. Probably the man with the greatest potential to do good of any man in the Old Testament — failed — because "he had himself to think about!"

Ronnie: It is a tragedy.

Gary: You remind me of Samson.

Ronnie: Oh now — really — you aren't comparing me to Samson? Have you seen my muscles lately? I'm hardly the world's strongest man!

Gary: I agree. You're not unusually strong — but you are "special" — you do carry a responsibility to your fellow-man and to God.

Ronnie: I don't understand you. There is nothing whatever special about me. I'm just an ordinary guy!

Gary: There are no ordinary guys in God's sight. Ronnie, He created you for a specific purpose. That makes you special. If you fail to develop your talents — if you fail to be the best that you can be — nations may not fall — but your fellow-men will be impoverished in some measure — and God's plan will be thwarted. That makes you responsible.

Ronnie: I don't understand you!

Gary: Ronnie, look. God has given us all different kinds of abilities. For a purpose. To Samson, He gave strength. To Solomon, He gave wisdom. To Antonio Stradivarius, He gave skill with wood.

Ronnie: Antonio who?

Gary: Antonio Stradivarius, the greatest violin maker in the world. Quite a different ability than Samson's. But important. That made him special. That gave him responsibility.

Ronnie: I remember hearing about him. Didn't George Eliot write a poem about Stradivarius that we had to read in English Lit?

Gary: Yes, he did. And in the poem, Stradivarius describes his feelings about his occupation of making violins which shows his understanding of what I am talking about. In his own way, Stradivarius was special. In his own way, he was responsible. Let's listen.

(Curtains open. Stradivarius is holding a violin. If no curtains, Stradivarius walks onstage with violin.)

Stradivarius (with strong Italian accent, if possible):

> But God be praised,
> Antonio Stradivarius has an eye
> That winces at false work and loves the true,
> With hand and arm that play upon the tool
> As willingly as any singing bird
> Sets him to sing his morning roundelay,
> Because he likes to sing and likes the song.

> When any master holds
> 'Twixt chin and hand a violin of mine,
> He will be glad that Stradivarius lived,
> Made violins, and made them of the best.
> The masters only know whose work is good:
> They will choose mine, and while God gives
>   them skill
> I give them instruments to play upon,
> God choosing me to help Him.

> 'Tis God gives skill,
> But not without men's hands: He could not make
> Antonio Stradivarius' violins
> Without Antonio.

> (George Eliot)

Gary: Stradivarius knew he was special. He knew he was responsible. He accepted both and made the world a better place.

Samson knew he was special. He knew he was responsible. He rejected both because he had himself to think about! And the world suffered.

Ronnie: And so did Samson.

Gary: Yes. We always suffer when we get outside God's will for our lives.

Ronnie: Why is that?

Gary: It's really very simple. When God created you, He gave you just the talents, just the aptitudes, just the dreams that, when developed, would fulfill a need He saw in the universe. Only when you fulfill that need will the highest skill of your talents, the highest development of your aptitudes, the highest dreams of your heart be complete. When you fall short of that best, you suffer. And — even though you repent and find a second chance with God, as Samson did, you know the highest plan is already shattered. You can never fulfill the need for which you alone were created.

Ronnie (thoughtfully): It's serious business to be special — to be responsible — isn't it?

Gary: Yes. Samson shrugged it off and brought tragedy. Antonio Stradivarius took it seriously and brought the world music. Ronnie, what will you do with your life? In your way, you, too, are special. In a way that only you can serve, you, too, are responsible to your fellow-man and to God. What will you do?

Ronnie (after a moment's reflection): I would like to pray.

(Gary remains on stool with head bowed. Ronnie slips to his knees, facing the audience. He does not bow his head. Be sure he speaks clearly, loudly enough to be heard throughout the room.)

Ronnie: O Lord, I thank You for making me special . . . for making me in such a way that I am not a Xerox copy of anyone else who has ever lived . . . for creating me for a special purpose in Your kingdom.

I understand that that kind of "specialness" makes me carry a heavy responsibility. Help me to be true to it. May I not look at the world's problems, as Samson did, shrug, and say: "I've got

49

myself to think about!'' Instead, O Lord, help me to determine, as Stradivarius did, to refine my ''specialness'' to such a point that I, too, may say:

> 'Tis God gives skill,
> But not without men's hands: He could not make
> The world better through Ronnie Ross
> Without Ronnie.
>   Amen.

(Ronnie holds pose.)
Invitation.

TRUE STORIES

Characters

Reggie: Teen-age boy with expressive voice
Rhonda: Teen-age girl with expressive voice
Joe: Teen-age boy

Setting

No setting necessary for this skit.

Costuming

All characters wear typical teen-age styles.

Properties

Reggie and Rhonda may sit on tall stools, if desired.

Skit

(Reggie and Rhonda enter and take their seats.)

Reggie: "Ernest Hemingway said that every true story ends in death. Well, this is a true story."

Rhonda: With these words, the beautiful television play *Brian's Song* begins. It tells of the friendship between two professional football players, Gale Sayers and Brian Piccolo. These two men played for the Chicago Bears; they were roommates on the road; they fought for the same position; they helped each other with plays; they pranked and laughed, played and worked. *Together.*

Reggie: Then tragedy struck. Brian Piccolo had cancer.

Piccolo was in the hospital when Sayers was given the George S. Halas — Most Courageous Player — Award. In a short halting speech, Sayers told the audience that he would give the trophy to his friend, Piccolo, because Brian "has that rare kind of courage that allows him to kid himself and his opponent — cancer."

Rhonda: Sayers, never a skilled speaker, drew on his greatest resources to add an epilogue to his speech of acceptance that night. "I love Brian Piccolo," he said, "and I'd like all of you to love

51

him, too. And tonight when you hit your knees, please ask God to love him."

Reggie: At the age of twenty-six, Brian Piccolo died. He left behind his wife, Joy, and three young daughters. He also left behind a great host of loving friends who remember him — not for how he died — but for how he lived. How he *did* live!

(There is pause here while Rhonda and Reggie seem to be thinking of "how he *did* live." Then Rhonda looks up.)

Rhonda: Ernest Hemingway said that every true story ends in death. Well, this is a true story.

Reggie: In a stable in Bethlehem, two thousand years ago, a small male infant was born. In the small village of Nazareth, He grew and developed into a strong gentle Man who went about the earth doing good. In the prime of life, He was betrayed by a man He had trusted. He was taken by force to a mock trial. There, a purple robe was put on His body, a crown of thorns was crushed into the tenderness of His brow, and scornful men bowed jeeringly before Him and rose to spit in His face.

Rhonda: He was taken to a hill called Golgotha. There He was placed on a wooden cross. And He died!

And with Him perished all that men hold dear;
Hope lay beside Him in the sepulcher,
Love grew corpse cold, and all things beautiful beside
    Died when He died!
But He rose!
And with Him hope arose, and Life and Light.
Men said, "Not Christ, but Death, died yesternight."
And joy and truth and all things virtuous
    Rose when He rose!*

Reggie: At the age of thirty-three, Jesus Christ died. Three days later, He rose from the dead and soon ascended into the heavens to sit at the right hand of the throne of God to make intercession for mankind. His death rent the curtain in the temple in two. . . . His death made it possible for man to return to God. . . . His death paid the penalty for the sin of the world.

Rhonda: Jesus Christ affected the human race, as has no other Person. Men of every era, of every country, of every tongue

---

*Author unknown.

remember Jesus Christ. Not only for the significance of His death — but for the Life He brought! What Life He *did* bring!

Reggie: Eternal life for all mankind.

Joe (entering): I've been listening to you two. It's a beautiful story — but can you prove it?

Rhonda (startled): Prove what?

Joe: Can you prove that Christ really *did* bring eternal life?

Reggie: It isn't proved, Joe! It can't be proved.
How can you prove a victory before
It's won?

Rhonda:
How can you prove a man who leads
To be a leader worth the following,
Unless you follow to the death, and out
Beyond mere death, which is not anything
But Satan's lie upon eternal life?

Reggie:
I bet my life
Upon one side in life's great war. I must,
I can't stand out. I must take sides. The man
Who is a neutral in this fight is not
A man . . .
I want to *live*, live out, not wobble through
My life somehow, and then into the dark.
I must have God . . .
I choose God as my leader, and I hold that He
Is good, and strong enough to work His plan
And purpose out to its appointed end.

Joe: But do you have evidence, man? I mean — on what do you base your choice?

Reggie:
I walk in crowded streets, where men
And women, mad with lust, loose-lipped, and lewd,
Go promenading down to hell's wide gates;
Yet have I looked into my mother's eyes
And seen the light that never was on sea
Or land, the light of love, pure love and true,
And on that love I bet my life . . .

Rhonda:

    I bet life on beauty, truth,
    And love! not abstract, but incarnate truth;
    Not beauty's passing shadow, but its self,
    Its very self made flesh — love realized.
    I bet my life on Christ, Christ crucified,
    Aye risen, and alive forevermore!

Joe: But you're still not proving anything! You offer some evidence of love — but not enough. You offer no answers to the questions of Good and Evil.

Rhonda:

    I ask not why the Evil,
    I ask not why the Good, both mysteries
    Remain unsolved, and both insoluble.
    I admit both are there, the battle set,
    And I must fight on this side or on that.
    I can't stand shiv'ring on the bank, I plunge
    Head first. . . .

Joe: Head first? Risking everything on a dare you cannot prove! All you know for sure is that He died —

Reggie: We remember Jesus Christ — not only for the significance of His death — but for the Life He brought! What *life* He did bring!

Rhonda:

    So through the clouds of Calvary — there shines
    His face; and I *believe* that Evil dies,
    And Good lives on, loves on, and conquers all . . .
    For God is Love. Such is my faith, and such
    My reasons for it, and I find them strong
    Enough. And you? You want to argue? Well,
    I can't. It's a choice. I choose the Christ.*

(Joe bows his head in meditation. Rhonda concludes on triumphant note. Reggie is caught in the grandeur of it with her. Both have tilted faces, eyes above audience. They all hold pose. The characters become merely background, holding the pose.)

    Invitation: Emphasize the words: "And *you?* It's your choice."

* Adapted for skit from "The Unutterable Beauty," by G. A. Studdart Kennedy. Used by permission of Hodder & Stoughton Limited, England.

TO EVERYTHING THERE IS A SEASON

Characters

Susan: Girl who has the ability to interpret expressively
Soloist

Setting

No setting required.

Costuming

Typical teen-age dress.

Properties

Slide projector, screen, slides.

Skit

(If curtains are available, Susan moves in front of closed curtains to perform. If curtain not available, she will perform onstage with the screen set up behind her.)

Susan (enters): I believe in God.
Because I am a child of the age
that asked life "Why?"
I wanted answers of my own.
I found answers on my own.
That is why
I believe in God.

When I first began my quest
I did not listen carefully to the words of my elders.
I did not respect advice from ancient masters.
I determined to find answers
on my own.

So I set out
And discovered that life
Is not fun and games . . .
It is for real . . .
It involves many things

That require from me my best
And if I do not give that best,
not only do I suffer,
but those about me!

I discovered that life required my careful thought.
I studied books that set down the philosophy
that I was merely a child of chance . . .
A lucky freak that grew unguided
From mud without a mind.
But something deep within me cried out
in protest.
I carefully weighed the evidence
Seeking for Truth until
Somehow I *knew,* unquestioningly, deep within
that I had more majesty than that!
I was more than a chemical body;
I was spirit —
made in the likeness of
— Who — but God?

I discovered that life required my honor.
I faced situations where right and wrong
confronted me
And I could choose.
I looked about and saw that I was alone.
I could choose the easy wrong over the hard right
And who would know?
But somehow I *knew*, unquestioningly, deep within
that Someone was there
placing me on my honor to choose the right.
But there was no one there that I could *see.*
Who could it be?
Who — but God?

I discovered that life required my perception.
I looked at men who denied God,
watched their little lives wrapped up in selfish pride
observed their faces etched so all the world
could know their sin.

And I looked at other men who walked with God,
watched their beautiful lives given freely in selflessness,
observed their faces etched so all the world
could see their love.
I carefully scrutinized the two types of men
For a difference
And *saw*.
And who could have made the difference?
Who — but God?
I discovered that life required a strength beyond my own.
I walked with a generation of youth
Who seemed determined to stand alone
without divine assistance.
One of the great moments of our literature
came in a book called *Love Story*.
It was the epic of two collegians,
Oliver and Jennifer,
Who found contentment in *their own* intellectual attainments;
Their own talent fulfillment,
Their own physical strength.
When they decided to marry;
They chose not a church, but a house;
They chose not Scripture, but sonnets;
They chose not God's blessing, but their own;
Because they did not believe in God
And would not be hypocrites.
Life moved along for them
Filled with the joy and vigor of their youth
Until a physician told Oliver
That Jennifer would die. . . .
And then the mind of this self-sufficient young man
Turned to God.*
Who could enable him to be strong for his beloved
In her last days?

*The movie version of *Love Story* did not play up this point. In case of challenge, see the book. Published by Signet Books (New American Library). See pages 109ff.

Who could give him the courage to walk "through the
valley of the shadow of death"?
Who — but God?
I believe in God.
Not because my church sings anthems
Not because my minister preaches sermons
Not because my parents have faith.
I believe in God
Because I walked a sincere road of reason
And found that life was Nowhere
Without Him. . . .
Life is not fun and games;
Life is for real.
And Who can give it meaning and purpose?
No one — but God!

(Lights begin to dim if stage is set with screen. Curtains open to
reveal screen, if curtains are used. Slides are shown as indicated.
Susan stands at side.)

Susan:

Life is not fun and games.
Life is for real
With varying seasons and purposes.
Who can make it all add up?
No one — but God.

Susan:	*Slides:*
To everything there is a season	*Fall scene*
And a time	*Winter scene*
To every purpose	*Spring scene*
Under the heaven	*Summer scene*
A time to be born	*Mother with baby*
And a time to die	*Cemetery monument*
A time to plant	*Hand placing seed in dirt*
And a time to pluck up That which is planted	*Hands plucking tomatoes from a vine*

58

A time to kill	*Rifle stuck in the ground; helmet hung on barrel head.*
And a time to heal	*Mother kissing child's finger*
A time to break down	*Children's blocks scattered*
And a time to build up	*Blocks erected into house*
A time to weep	*Crying child*
And a time to laugh	*Girl laughing*
A time to mourn	*Somber-faced older lady with Bible; she is sitting in rocking chair*
And a time to dance	*Group of laughing teens*
A time to cast away stones	*Building being torn down*
And a time to gather stones together	*House under construction*
A time to embrace	*Couple at marriage altar*
And a time to refrain from embracing	*Same couple as above: girl washing dishes; boy drying.*
A time to get	*Man presenting beaming boy a baseball trophy*
And a time to lose	*Man presenting a different beaming boy with baseball trophy while first boy looks on with wistful eyes*
A time to keep	*Little girl holding small puppy*
And a time to cast away	*Same little girl fighting off larger dog (same color and breed as puppy preferably)*
A time to rend	*Small boy in tree looking in amazement at large hole in trouser knee*
And a time to sew	*Mother mending trouser knee*
A time to keep silence	*Listening congregation in church*
And a time to speak	*Lady talking with another lady – Pointing to Scripture in the Bible*
A time to love	*Mother cuddling a small boy*

And a time to hate	*Discarded beer can*
A time of war	*Couple arguing with each other*
And a time of peace	*Children saying bedtime prayers*
He hath made everything beautiful in His time	*Lakeside scene*
And God hath promised	*Sallman's picture of Christ*

To be with us when we walk
through sunshine

And when we walk through
storms

Life is not fun and games.
Life is for real
With varying seasons and purposes
Who can give us the strength for its demands?
No one — but God.

(With total focus beamed on the slide, a male soloist sings offstage: "You'll Never Walk Alone."*)

Susan:
I believe in God.
Not because my church sings anthems
Not because my minister preaches sermons
Not because my parents have faith.
I believe in God
Because I walked a sincere road of reason
And found that life is not fun and games
Life is for real
With varying seasons and purposes
Too big for me to face alone.
But *Who* can walk with me and give

---

*The song, "You'll Never Walk Alone," was written by Richard Rodgers and Oscar Hammerstein II for their musical *Carousel*. It may be obtained in sheet music at your local music store or the score of the musical may be obtained from your library.

me the strength I need?
Who can guarantee I will never walk alone?
No one — but God.

(Focus holds on the slide of Christ. Leader, take over.)